The Child in Me

Words and Art by Oshri Liron Hakak

Story Inspiration and Guided Meditation
by Orly Altaras

BUTTERFLYON BOOKS

First Edition
Copyright © 2024, by Oshri Liron Hakak and Orly Altaras
All Rights Reserved

The Child in Me
Written and Illustrated by Oshri Liron Hakak and Orly Altaras

Published by Butterflyon Books
Los Angeles
ISBN 979-8-9868755-6-9

With gratitude for my beloved friend, James Mihaley,
and for children... those in their early years,
and those innocents within us, no matter our age.

With gratitude to Wendy Kashefi for helping to connect us and
so many others to our inner children and to our wisdom guides.

The Child in Me

All of us hold an inner child,
no matter how old we are,
no matter wild,
or unwild.

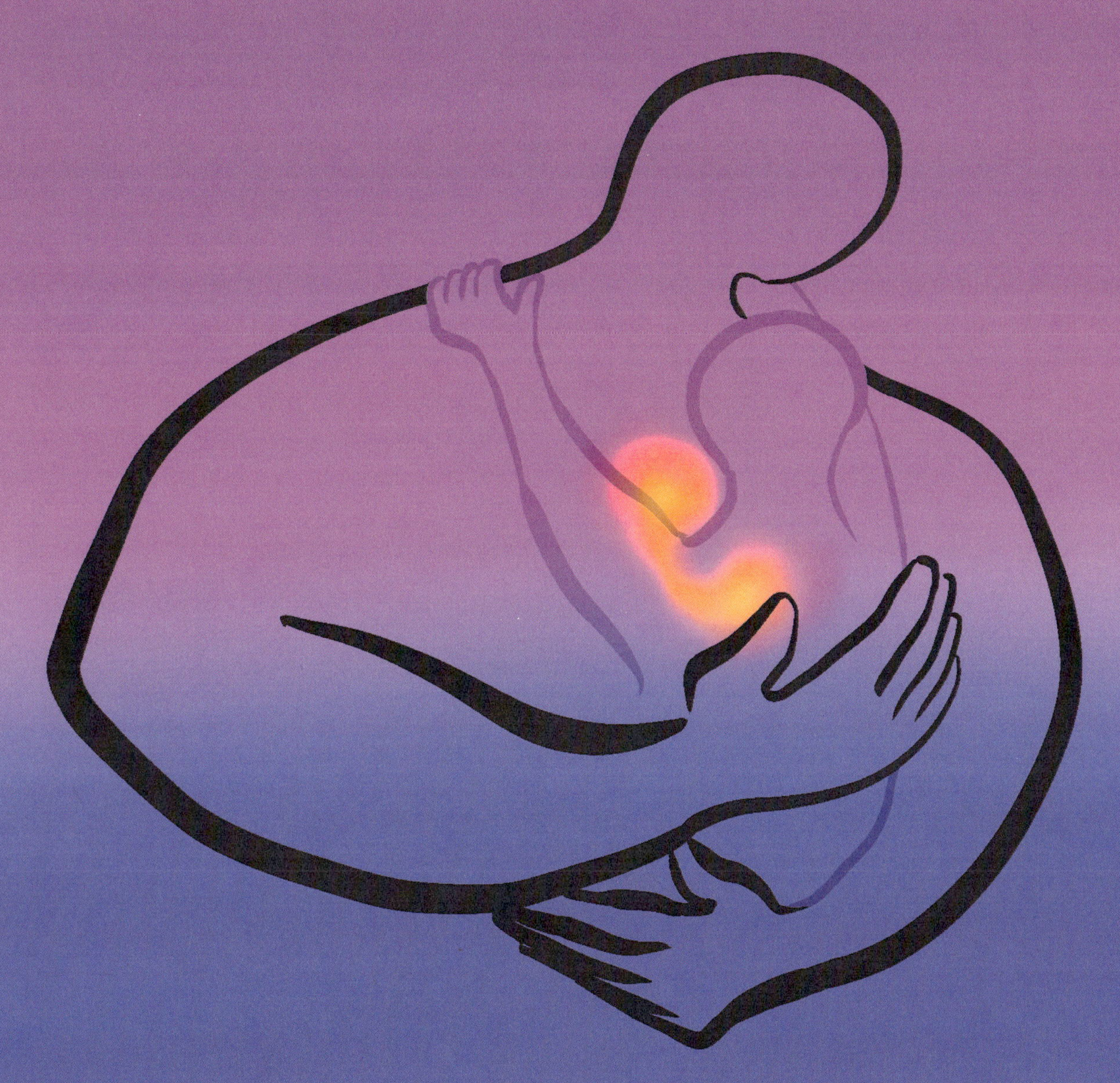

A grown-up who's bossy or mean
may often be steered by their inner teen,
or even an infant in the process of wean.

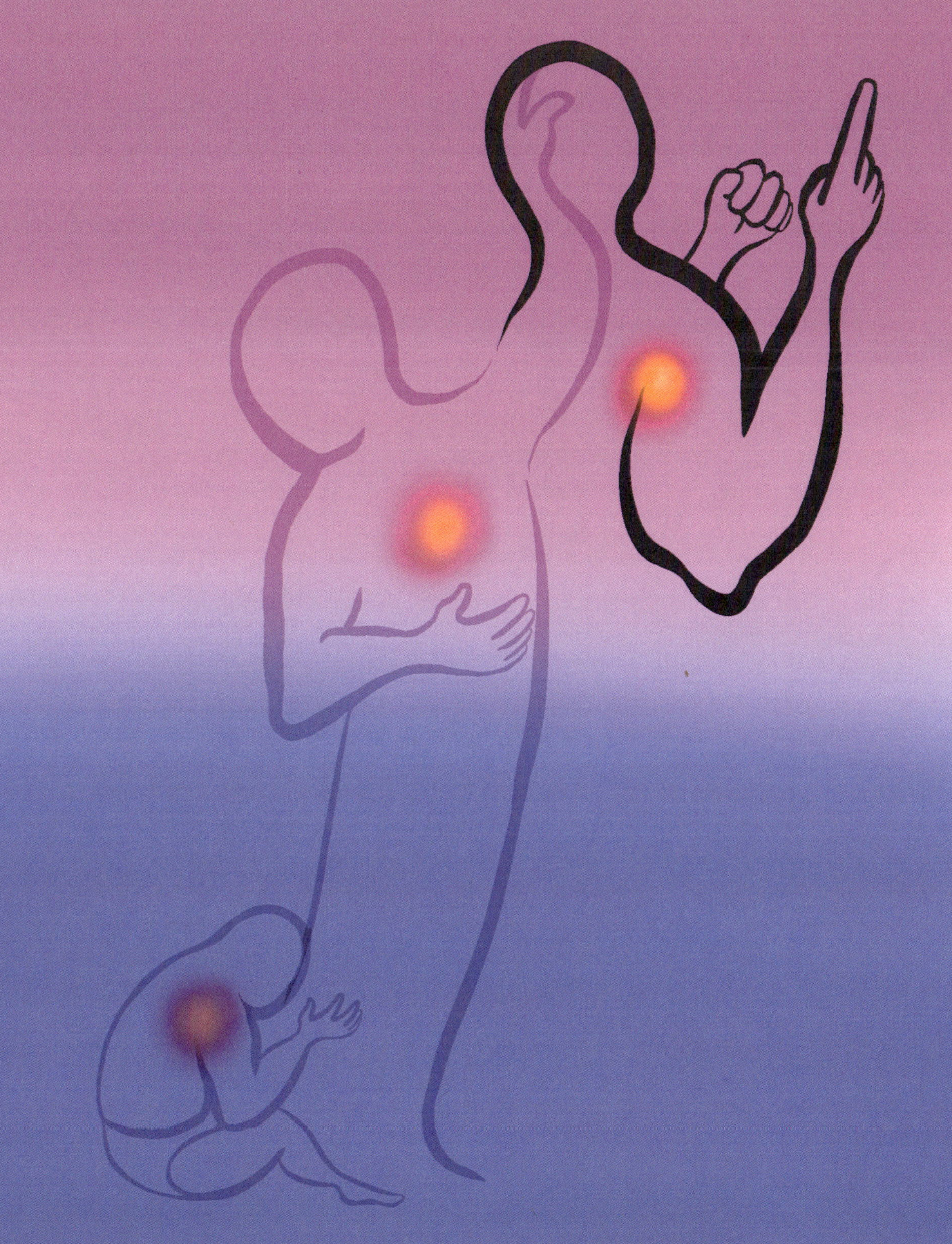

Hey there, fella, all angry-macho!
With caring eyes, I gently watch you…

Machoing can be with muscles or with brains, too...
any time people try to control a people-zoo.

Maybe something happened to that child inside,
something big, long ago…
or lots of small, hurtful things
that left them needing to control the show.

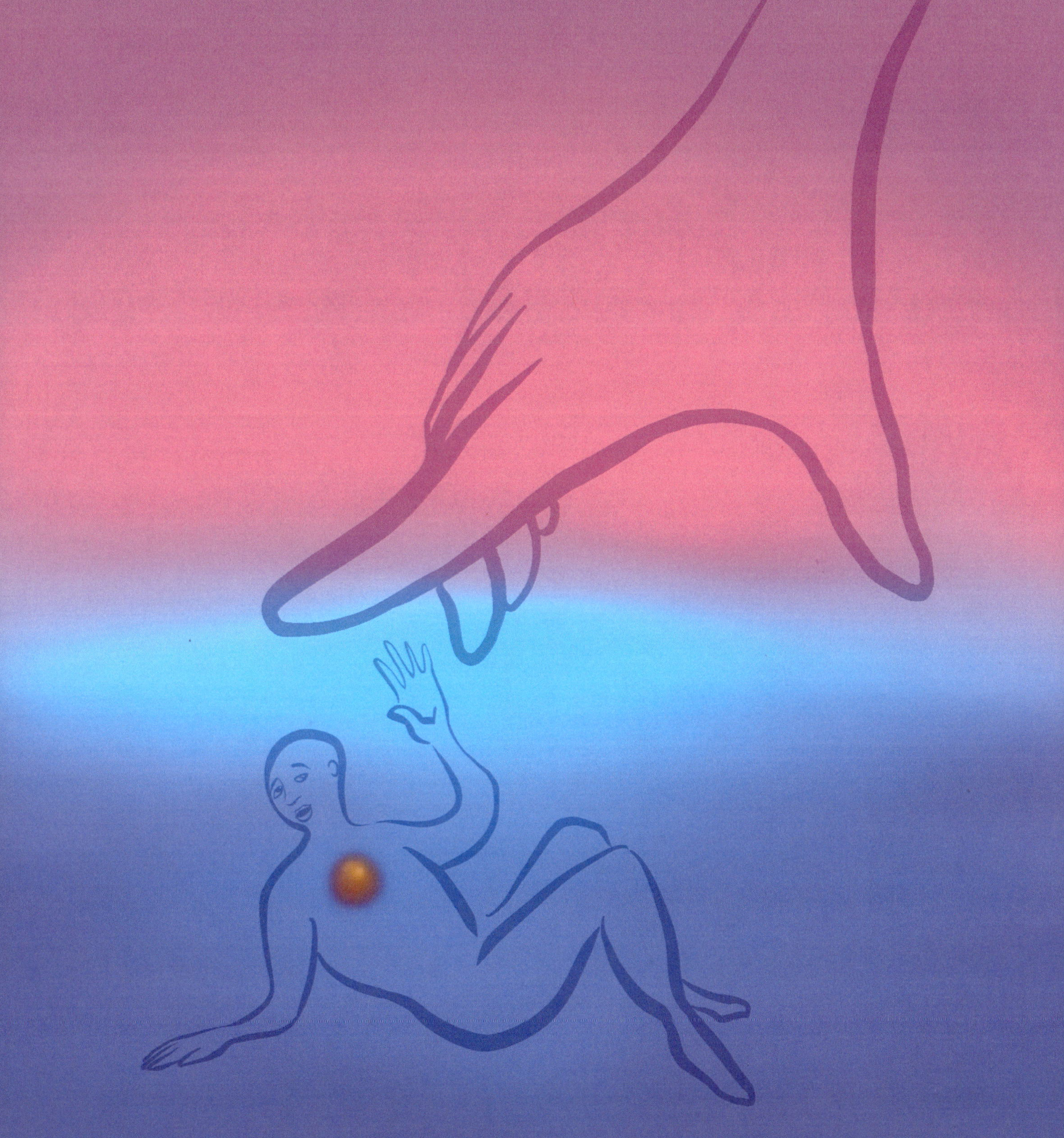

Good news is we can help the child inside,
and, earning enough trust,
they may be happy to just come along for the ride.

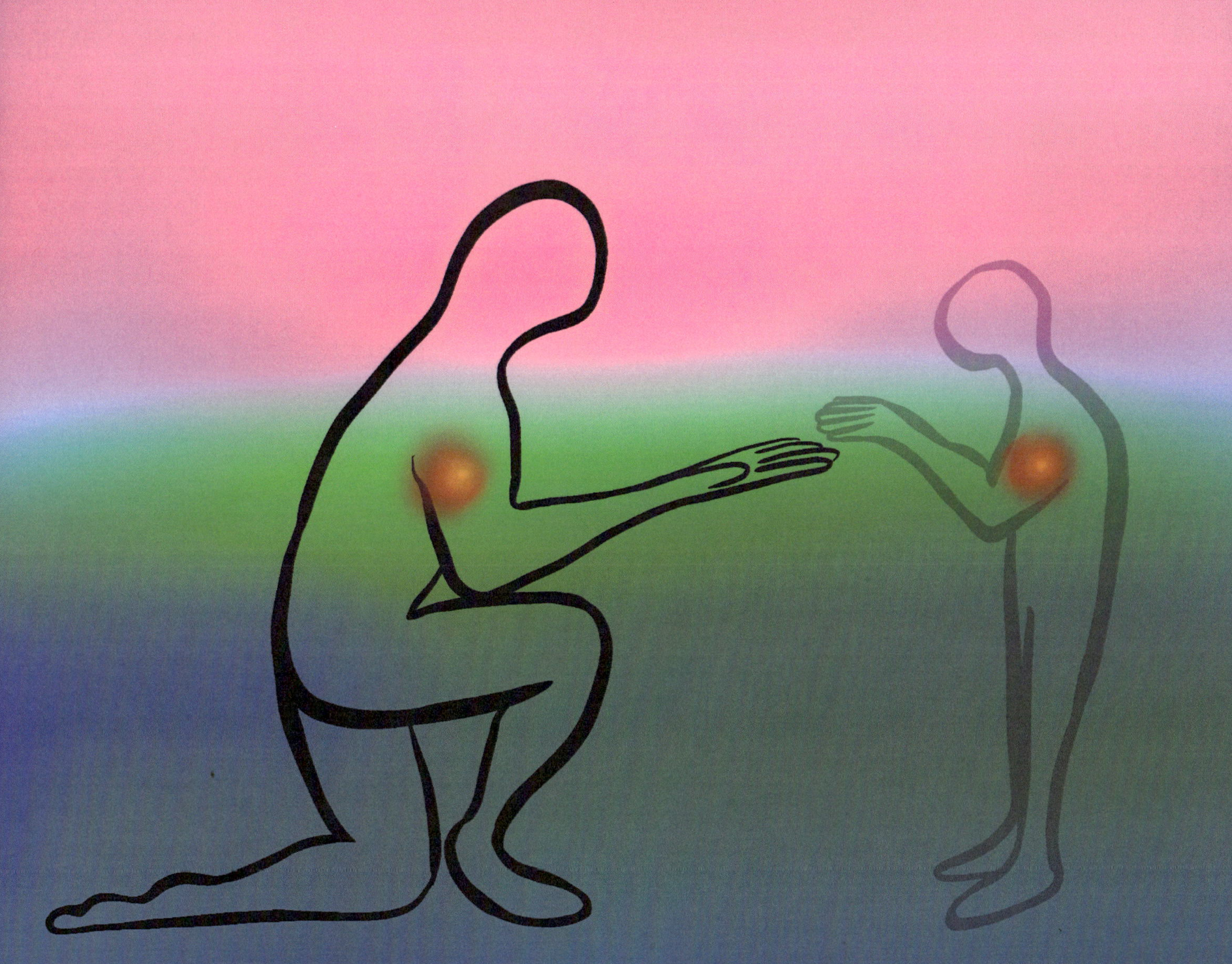

We can close our eyes and search our bodies to remember,
taking deep breaths to feel any lingering, hurting ember.

Remembering that ember can also fuel our light,
with our heart's lamp we can approach the child in us who's
tugging in fright.

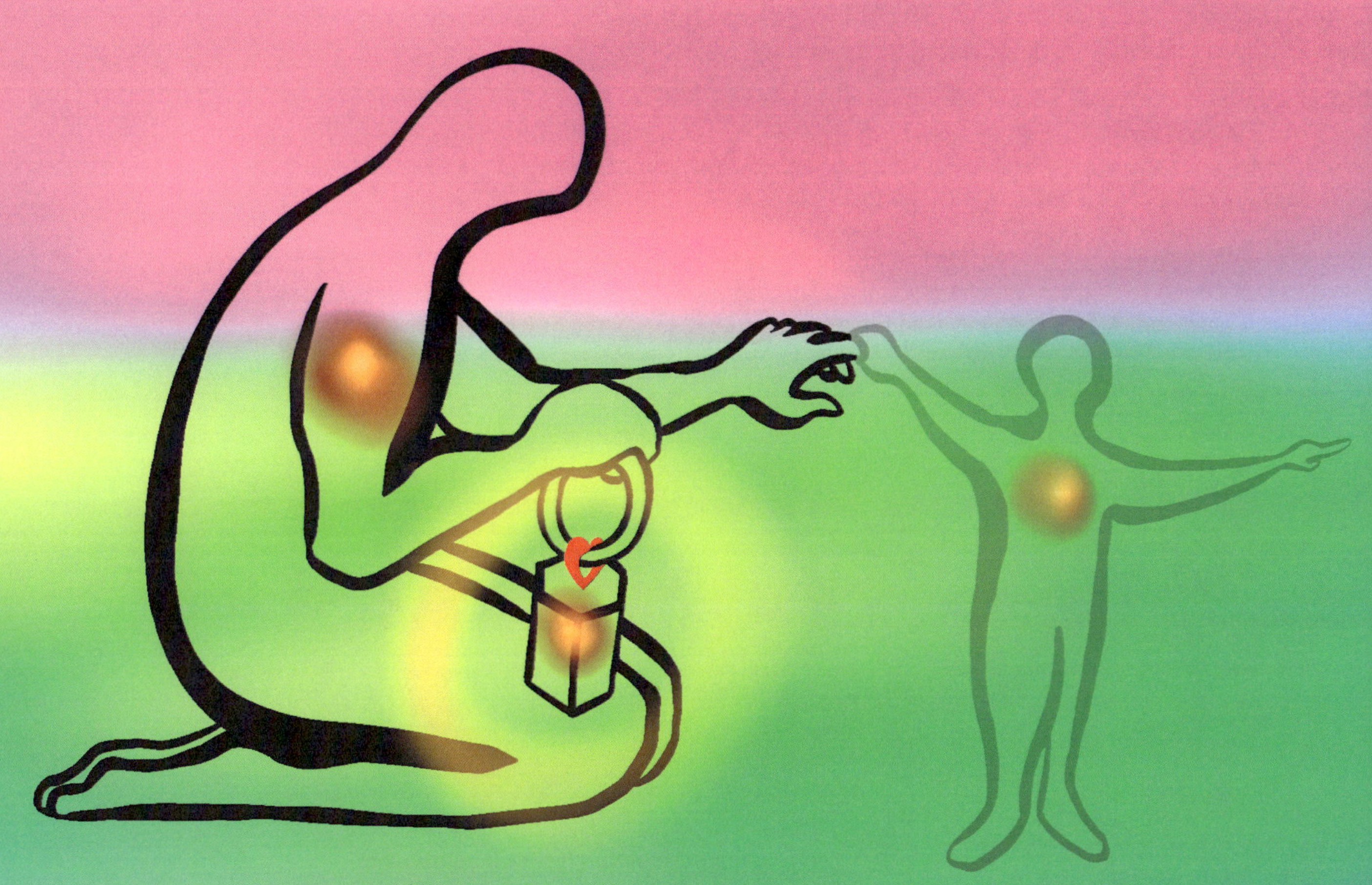

Telling them, "I know… it was awful, it wasn't right…
but stay with me, Love, now I embrace you tight."

Holding their hand we can give them comfort,
saying, "I'm so sorry, my Dear, you were so injured."

"I see you, I hear you, I feel you,
and now I have the strength to hold you."

Now slowly see if the child can be soothed and guided,
"I love you and appreciate that our lives coincided."

Remember when you go out there,
it's not the adults of whom we must sometimes beware—
but our inner untended children who lacked the right kind of care.

It's okay to judge, but don't let your judge play boss or nanny,
when your situation might be better resolved
embodying a gentle granny.

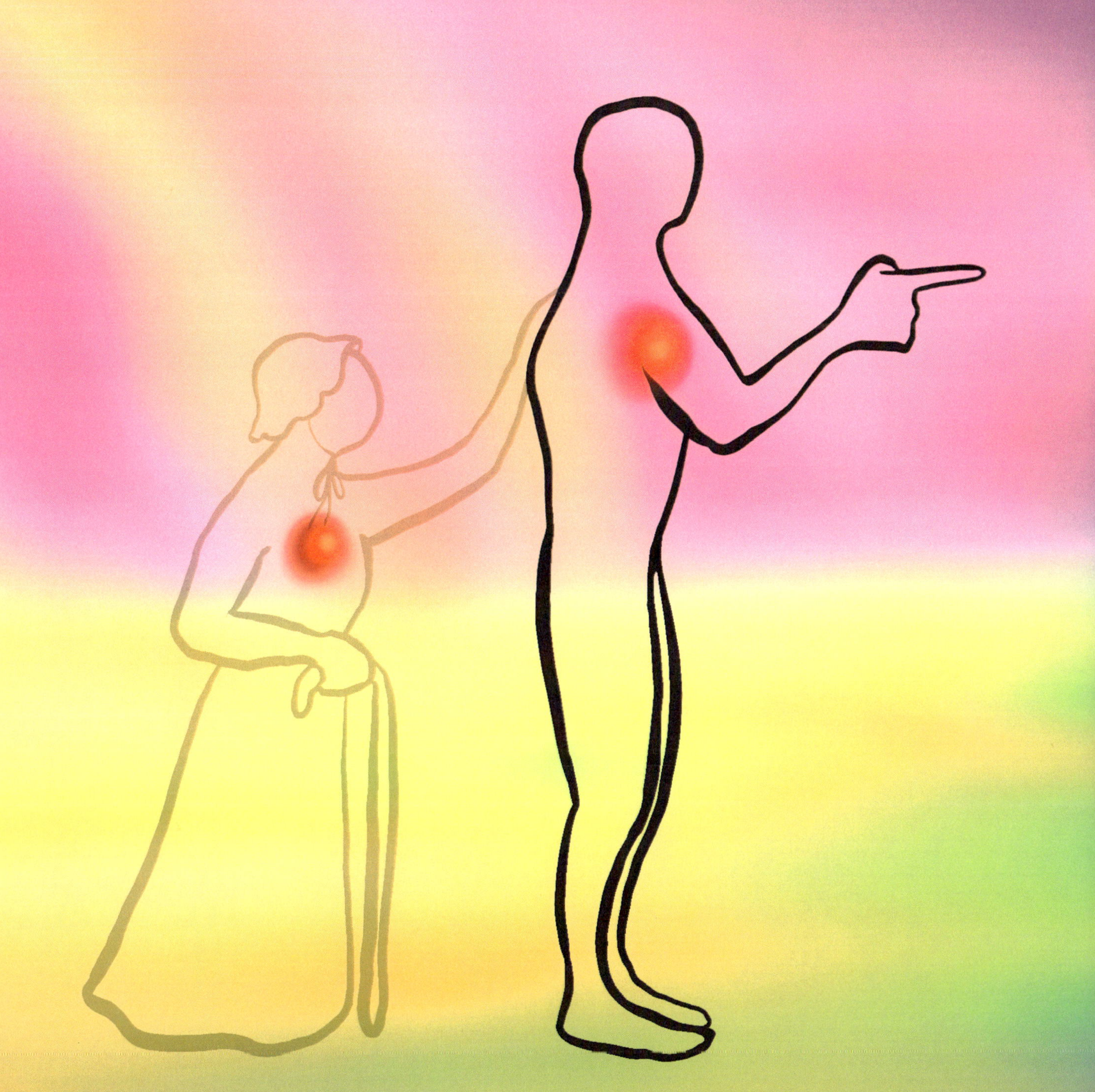

Yes... that's right... no matter our age,
we have not only a child in us,
but also wise and loving grandparent-guides
to help tend to our fuss...

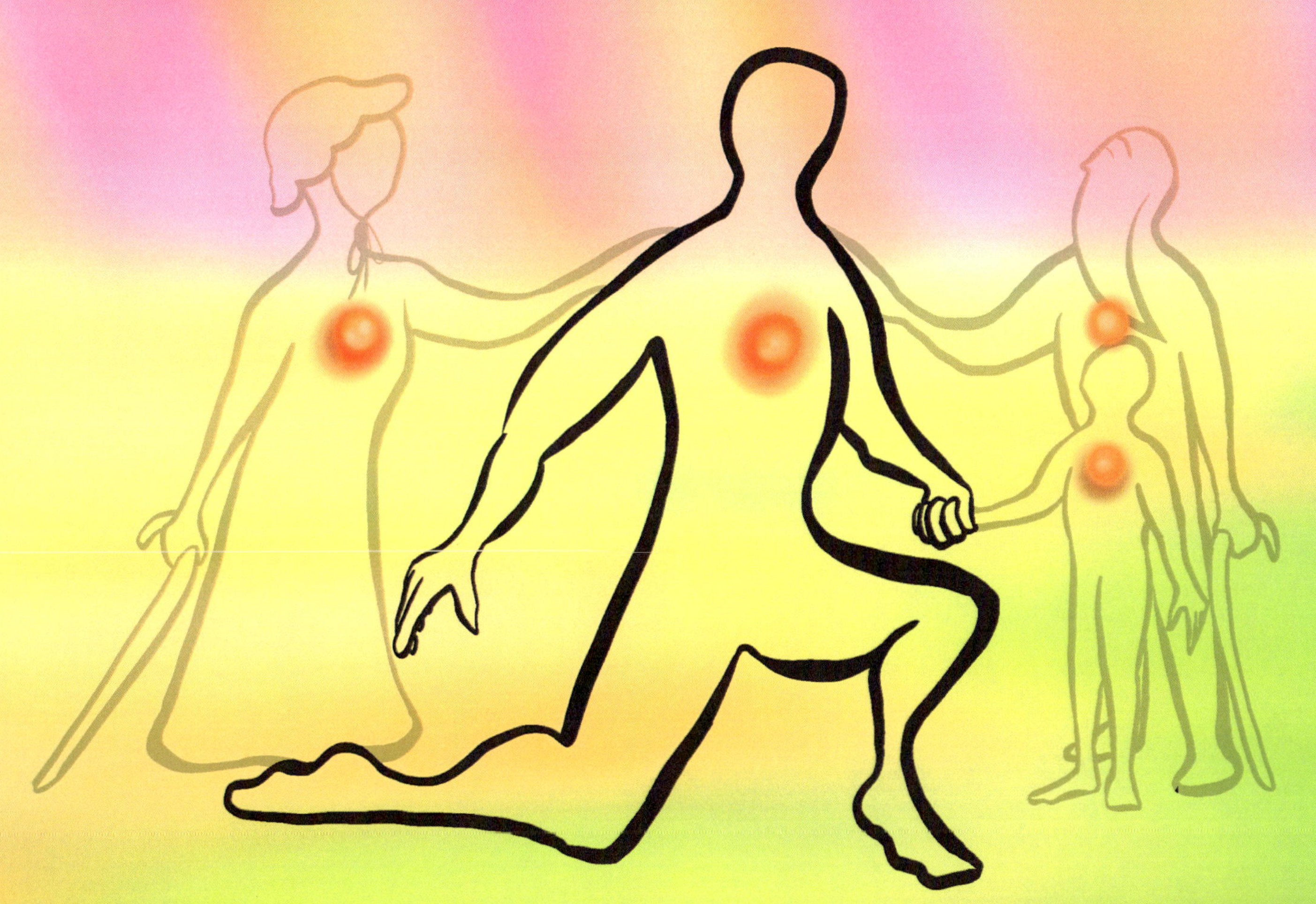

We can reach our ancestors and our aged future-selves,
their seasoned knowing flowing from where the source of wisdom dwells.
They've had time to deepen into healing,
love, fulfillment, strength and meaning.

Imagine now the homes that might be healed,
the joy we might together yield.

Everyone, closing our eyes,
making a strongly tender decree…
Saying, "Dear Child in Me, you're safe and free."

"I offer you this inward hug,
We'll sip together from a cozy mug."

"All your pain I deeply honor,
name it, write it, sing it, paint it, dance it, exhale it...
over time we'll learn to be calmer."

"Child, you sit at the roots of this precious life's tree...
Dear Child in Me, you're safe and free."

MEND

A Guided Meditation for Healing the Child in Me
by Orly Altaras

Record yourself reading this meditation out loud. Be sure to read it slowly and with plenty of space for slow, deep breathing and contemplation. Then, listen back to the recording, practicing connecting with the child in you.

Begin by getting into a comfortable position.

When you are ready, close your eyes. Begin by tuning into your breath and your body.

Allow yourself to relax and take a deep breath in. As you get comfortable, notice any tension in your body and release those areas that are calling for your attention.

Relax the eyes, forehead, shoulders. Relax your jaw. Take another deep breath in and exhale. Relax your abdomen, legs and feet.

Remind yourself that you are in a safe space and all that you need is with you at this time.

As you take another deep breath in, imagine a white beam of light entering the top of your head & slowly running down, filling your entire body… from the top of your head, through your face, feeling the white light beaming through you, down through your neck, throat and shoulders, through your arms, fingertips, filling your chest all the way down to your feet and surrounding you with love and protection…

Breathe in the white light, expanding your body, and with every exhale, release any tension and discomfort. Let your body be enveloped in this white light, envision and experience it within you and surrounding you.

Take another deep breath in and exhale.

As you enter this protective space, and as you go inward, nourished by this healing white light, imagine yourself standing on a path in a white cloud that surrounds you and slowly opens up and clears with each step forward that you take. Walk slowly on this path, this corridor of light, and you begin to see a silhouette that becomes clearer with each step forward.

As you come nearer, you see that the form is of you as a child.

Trust whatever version of younger-you appears, and have clarity about what age is present. It may be different each time you do this. The important thing is practicing trust within this inner vision.

Continuing to approach, feel into your heart. You may want to reach out your arms with openness (physically or in your mind), and let them sense you are here for them, that they are safe. Continue to breathe slowly and deeply.

As you come closer and closer, feel the white light surround both of you. You may feel a need to hold and hug this young version of you. Honor it.

Spend a few breaths absorbed in and absorbing the child in you. Let them know that you are here for them. That you love them. That it is safe for them to express how they feel with you. That you are here for them...

Become aware of how they feel as you extend your love to them. Let them share with you their feelings at this time.

Feel the sensations of their emotions.

They may have a feeling they want to express to you. Let it emerge. This may be an emotion they didn't know how to handle or it may be an emotion they wish for you to feel. Sense deeply into the sensation they are sharing with you. Listen to them and tell them you know how they feel, and let them feel your love.

Let your child version of you know "It's OK to feel what you feel". Tell them you love them and accept them and understand.

Communicate with them from a place of wisdom and understanding.

If it feels right, help unpack with them the circumstances that make them feel this way. It could be that they feel as though no one is noticing their feelings or taking into consideration how they feel about a situation which is of out of their control. Stay curious, open, and caring.

Encourage your young self to ask questions. Share your answers as honestly as you can. Acknowledge and make them feel safe with how they feel. Affirm to them that you understand what they want. Share your compassionate and contemplative reflections with them, perhaps why something they desire is not fulfilled, or a deeper understanding of why something didn't go the way they wanted...

Tell them you hear them.

Tell them you love them and that you will always love them.

Say to them, "Thank you for sharing this experience with me. I honor you and hear you. I appreciate you as you are no matter what, and your feelings are meaningful and important to me."

Now, ask your inner child if there is anything else they want you to know at this time, and let them whisper it to you. Trust what you sense, hear or feel.

Let them know you love them, that they are safe, and that you will always love them.

See them feeling lighter and freer.

Embrace each other and say thank you to each other as you get ready to come back into your physical presence. You wave to one another other, knowing you can always meet like this again.

Now... slowly return to your body.

See yourself still surrounded by this white light, noticing how you are feeling.

Feel gratitude in your heart.

Slowly take a deep breath in, and exhale knowing you can always return here if you wish. Feel the energy of love encompass you.

Remain in your breath, inhaling, lifting your shoulders and releasing, and exhaling with a sigh. Move your fingers and toes, hands and feet, legs and arms, slowly... and when you are ready, open your eyes back to your present moment.

Thank You NAMI Westside Los Angeles

Thank you to NAMI Westside Los Angeles for supporting the creation of this book. NAMI Westside Los Angeles is a part of NAMI, a grassroots mental health advocacy organization that offers free education, programming and support for people who are struggling with mental health conditions, as well as for those who are supporting loved ones experiencing challenging mental health conditions.

Mental health for anyone is good for everyone. No matter who you are and where you are, you are not alone. You can find out more about NAMI and its offerings at NAMIWLA.org.

About the Creators of This Book

Oshri Hakak

Oshri loves to make art, music and books to aid people and communities in our individual and collective healing journeys.

You can find more of Oshri's books on ButterflyonBooks.com . His art and music are also on Instagram—@oshrihakak .

Orly Altaras

Orly is a Psychic Medium and spiritual teacher who connects with loved ones in spirit and delivers messages of comfort and guidance from source. She helps you to tap into your soul's innate abilities and uses tools and resources so that you can live and create your heart's desires with ease. The love between people is her soul's work. You can find her on Instagram- @laraandlou .

More Titles by Butterflyon Books

ButterflyonBooks.com

Books for 12 Years Old and Up

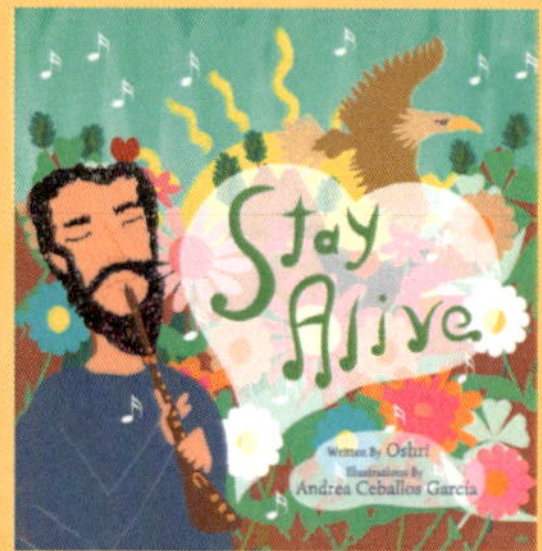

Children's Books for All Ages

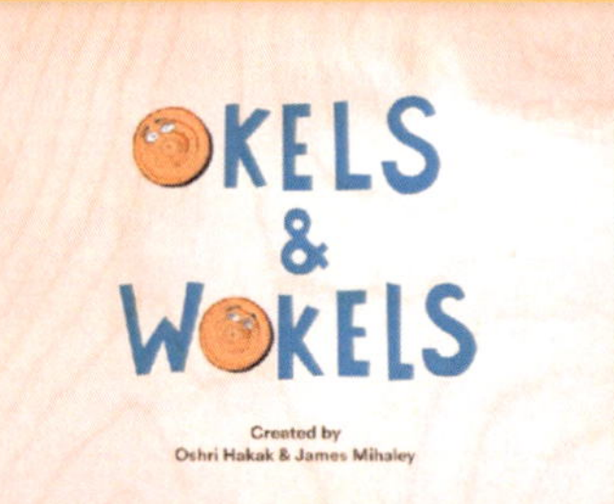

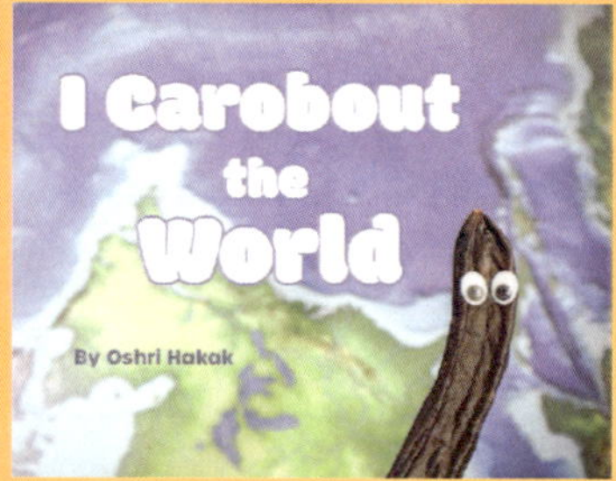

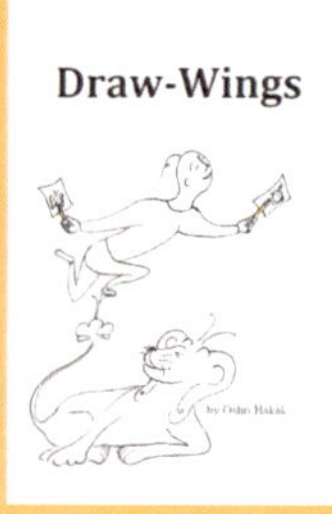

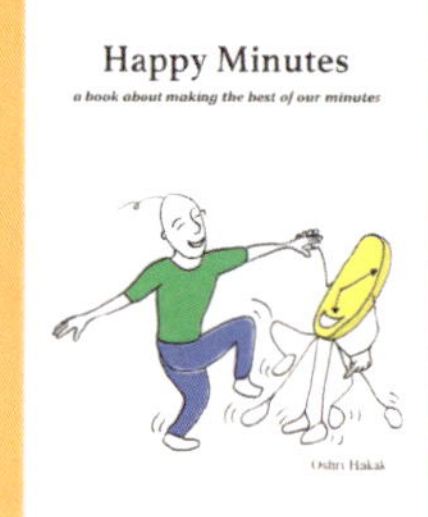

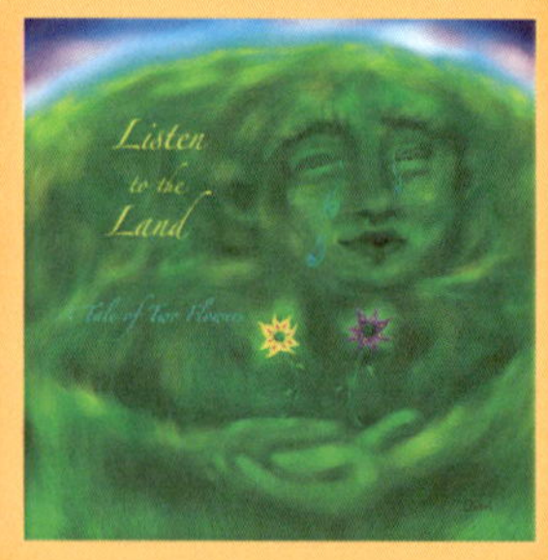